hurt

NOTES ON TORTURE IN A MODERN DEMOCRACY

KRISTIAN WILLIAMS

Hurt

Notes on Torture in a Modern Democracy

by Kristian Williams

Published by

Microcosm Publishing
112C S. Main St.
Lansing, KS 66043-1501
&
636 SE 11th Ave.
Portland, OR 97214

For a catalog, go to
www.microcosmpublishing.com

ISBN 978-1-934620-64-9

First Edition, May 2012

This is Microcosm #76086

Edited by Adam Gnade
Designed by Joe Biel
Fonts by Ian Lynam
Cover by Matt Gauck

Contents

4. Introduction:
A Question of Democracy

Part One: Personal Reflections

9. "Confronting Horror: Writing About Torture." *New Politics*. Winter 2008

Part Two: Media Silence and Public Opinion

12. "Interview by Gyozo Nehez: Amerikai Modszerek: Kinzas Es Az Vralom Logikaja." *Indymedia.hu*. October 22, 2006

17. "Against Self-Censorship: Countering CBS's Critics." *Extra!* August 2004

20. "Keeping the State's Secrets: Media and Government in the United States." *The World Today*. February 2006

Part Three: Torture, Democracy, and Inequality

25. "Interview by David Cunningham: Prisons, Torture, and Imperialism." *Anti-Poverty Committee Prison Justice Journal*. Winter 2006

28. "Hidden Torture, False Democracy." *International Socialist Review*. September-October 2008

43. "Second Thoughts on Psychological Torture." *Make/Shift*. Spring-Summer 2009

Part Four: Prison Abolition

48. "Interview by Dave Mazza: Turn of the Imperialist Screw." *Portland Alliance*. June 2006

51. "Caging Race and Gender: *Are Prisons Obsolete?*" *Against the Current*. January-February 2005

53. "Critical Resistance at 10: Addressing Abolition, Violence, Race, and Gender." *Against the Current*. March-April 2009

Part Five: Conclusions and Synopses

58. "What Anarchism Contributes to Our Understanding of Torture." *Social Anarchism*. 2008-2009

60. "Five Theses on Violence." *The Body as a Site of Discrimination: Exploring and Resisting Body-Based Oppressions*. April 17, 2009

63. About the Author

Introduction:
A Question of Democracy

I started writing about torture almost by accident.

I was just finishing my first book, *Our Enemies in Blue*, when CBS went public with the Abu Ghraib photos. Those pictures, showing American soldiers smiling and giving the "thumbs-up" as they abuse, humiliate, and terrify helpless prisoners, did not surprise me in the least. But the media's handling of the controversy—in particular, the repeated insistence that "This is not how we do things in America"—was more than I could tolerate.

That sense of dissonance, the clash between what I knew to be true and what we were told in the news, became the impetus for my second book, *American Methods: Torture and the Logic of Domination*. At the time, I wanted to show that the torture at Abu Ghraib was not anomalous, but was instead a predictable result of some of the basic features of our society—racism, imperialism, male dominance, and the state.

*   *   *

That the United States practices torture is now, I think, beyond dispute. What this fact means, however—what it says about our society—ought to be the subject of more controversy than it has been.

A major conclusion pushed by the essays in this collection is that the United States is not, in any sense that matters, a genuine democracy. Attention to our government's practice of torture shows not just how undemocratic the U.S. is, but also provides some idea as to the ways in which it is undemocratic. The institutions using torture tend to be the most repressive and least accountable parts of the state, and the uses to which torture is put broadly illustrate the distribution of power in our society. In particular, torture reveals the imperialist nature of America's foreign policy objectives, and of its super-power position in the global system; and, it reflects the stratification of our domestic society along the lines of race, class, gender, citizenship, and so on.

The   subtitle   of   this publication—"Notes on Torture in a Modern   Democracy"—is   therefore deeply, bitterly, ironic.

Where   torture   persists, democracy is lacking.

*   *   *

On the whole, the essays collected in this pamphlet were written alongside, or shortly after, *American Methods*—during George W. Bush's second term, 2005-2009.

In 2008, Barack Obama was elected president, largely thanks to popular discontent concerning the Bush administration and its various crimes. Obama's candidacy sold us a slogan of hope, but his presidency has only delivered disappointment. Despite some encouraging pronouncements early on, Obama's torture policy, in most respects, represents a refined continuation of Bush's.

Even Obama's grandest gesture—ordering the closure of the Guantánamo Bay prison—has come to nothing. In truth, that is just as well, since Obama still adheres to many of those policies that made Gitmo such an embarrassment in the first place. Like Bush, Obama asserts the military's right to detain suspects indefinitely and without trial. And like Bush, Obama is pushing ahead with Military Commission prosecutions, even allowing the admission of evidence gained by using torture. Most telling, Obama seems to be making Bagram Air Base the new Guantánamo: administration lawyers argue that domestic courts have no jurisdiction over operations in Afghanistan, even as the military uses the base to hold prisoners captured outside of any war zone.

Furthermore, Obama has made it clear that he will continue the practices that have traditionally insulated presidents from accountability. Though he's allowed the prosecution of a few low-level functionaries, he has refused to investigate those who designed and authorized Bush's torture programs. He has refused to release new evidence—including Abu Ghraib-style photos and documents showing Bush's authorization for secret prisons. And he has steadfastly maintained the secrecy surrounding the extraordinary rendition program and the military's interrogation techniques. The administration has also vigorously fought lawsuits brought by those who were tortured under these programs, citing (variously) Bush-era policies, the state secrets doctrine, and the separation of powers.

All of this, of course, is exactly what we should have expected. Torture did not begin with Bush, and there was no reason to think that it would end with him. As I argue in these essays, an end to torture will require more than any election can provide. It will require something like a revolution.

To end torture, our society must become, at long last, a democracy.

*   *   *

Democracy is one of those permanently contested notions. As George Orwell observed long ago, when we call something democratic, it is usually because we mean to praise it. After that, the arguments begin.

The word "democracy" means, etymologically, "rule of the people." Unfortunately, the word has been sullied by its long association with the state. But, as John Gardner pointed out in a recent issue of the *London Review of Books*, "the rule of the people is not the rule of the government." In fact, they are opposites.

My own view is that the central norm underlying democratic principles is one of autonomy. If we believe that people should be, so far as possible, free from the intrusions of others, then that means that we have to trust them to arrange their own affairs. They have to make their own decisions. And if freedom is not just a special privilege enjoyed by some elite caste, then it follows that in decisions affecting multiple people everyone should have an equal say in how those decisions are made. That suggests a model of decision-making that is egalitarian, participatory, and local.

In practice it would mean that neighborhoods should be controlled by the people who live in them; farms, factories, and shops, by the people who work in them; schools, by the students and the teachers. In other words, it would mean an end to the rule of landlords, businessmen, politicians, bureaucrats, and police.

Real democracy would be not parliamentarian, but anarchistic. Where the people rule, there are no rulers.

*   *   *

Hurt opens on a personal note, with a meditation on my experience writing about torture. The following sections then focus on the media's complicity in government crimes, the connection between torture and social stratification, the case for the abolition of prisons, and the conceptual centrality of the state. Short interviews are used to introduce each of the main topics.

I pose the question of democracy most directly in the longest essay of this set, "Hidden Torture, False Democracy." That piece, together with the one following it ("Second Thoughts on Psychological Torture"), make up my critique of Darius Rejali's impressive and voluminous study *Torture and Democracy*. Where Rejali argues that the Western democracies—including the United States—have been the main innovators in torture over the last hundred years, I accept his facts, but challenge his analysis. Specifically, I scrutinize his definitions for the two crucial concepts—democracy, in the first essay; torture, in the second—and I use the evidence he presents to highlight the relationship between torture and inequality.

At the end of the collection, I push the question of the democracy further, to the issue of the state itself. First, I make a case for approaching the study of torture from an anarchist perspective. Then, in "Five Theses on Violence," I draw out in some detail an argument about the nature of the state, the political uses of violence, and the possibilities for resistance. These two pieces serve as a kind of distillation of *Hurt*'s overall argument.

*   *   *

I am grateful to Gyozo Nehev, Dave Mazza, and David Cunningham for allowing me to reprint the interviews they conducted. I am also grateful to the editors of the various periodicals that published these articles, and to the crew at Microcosm, for their comments and their guidance.

I owe further thanks to a great many friends who read early drafts and offered beneficial critical remarks; with the passage of time, I have largely forgotten who, precisely, commented on what, so this particular debt will just have to be marked "to whom it is due." The exception is Emily-Jane Dawson, always my first reader. Thanks.

Kristian Williams
Portland, Oregon
August 2010

Part One:
Personal Reflections

Confronting Horror: Writing About Torture

(*New Politics*, Winter 2008)

I did not dream of being tortured.

But I did dream of being caged, of being bound and blindfolded, of being kept cold and naked in a small steel box. I dreamed of terrible footsteps, always approaching, and the chilling sound of metal clanging against metal. I dreamed of endless screams, and of shadows that stretched toward me, and of hands holding instruments that I could never quite see.

The dreams ended, always, before the pain could become real. But that is a small matter. The fear was real enough.

*   *   *

I spent a little less than a year researching and writing my book *American Methods*—or, a little more than a year if you count the time spent on revisions. The book examines the U.S. government's use of torture—in war, in prison, and by proxy. My research led me to read scores of human rights reports, hundreds of pages of government documents, countless newspaper articles, and numerous books on the history and practice of torture, international law, global politics, and rape. I learned a whole new vocabulary—"hooding," "monstering," "stress positions," "*falaka*," "strip cells," "rendition," "waterboarding," "the Palestinian hanging." And I became acquainted with all variety of imaginative new uses for radiators, pliers, sandbags, broom handles, wire brushes, and typewriter covers.

At the beginning, I was impossibly naive. Not that I believed our government's official line—that torture is rarely practiced and never condoned—but I thought I could immerse myself in the subject for months and not suffer because of it.

I should have known better. I had already written one book about state violence, and I clearly remembered weeping at my keyboard, searching for words with which to describe the deep and abiding hate that could produce the murders of the civil rights workers Andrew Goodman, Michael Schwerner, and James Chaney. I remembered the chill I felt typing out "death squad" as I wrote about the assassination of Fred Hampton. And still—I thought I could confront our practices of torture without sharing in the spiritual wreckage that those practices have wrought.

I assumed that my anger would protect me from the worst facts that I could be made to face. I was wrong, in part because anger cannot—and should not—diminish sorrow, or shame, or impotent loathing. But I expected to stare into the abyss without the abyss staring into me.

*   *   *

Pain never featured directly in my dreams. I did not see the torturers themselves, or their instruments. It was the fear—the terror—that forced me awake, gasping and sweat-soaked, in the middle of the night. And when I woke the fear stayed with me. The world felt uncomfortably small. The very idea of safety seemed brittle and thin; order was an obscene joke.

I gradually learned how to keep the nightmares at bay. They came in a cycle, and I labored to recognize it. So when I noticed that I was having trouble sleeping, before the dreams became too intense, I would shift my focus from research to writing. I would put away, for a time, whatever I was reading and try instead to get my thoughts in order, to translate my dread into written language. I built a wall with words. And as long as I kept writing, my anxiety would fade, my nightmares would cease. If writing could not restore the feeling of safety, it could at least shore up my confidence in my own quiet sanity. Such, I suspect, is a major reason why I write—to confront, understand, articulate, and in a very limited way, to control that which I fear.

But I have also lost something, which could not rightly be called innocence and may be rather closer to faith. For I have come to see that the human spirit is not indomitable. It can be so thoroughly crushed that freedom and dignity disappear. They can be blotted out, surviving not even as ideals or aspirations. In one way, I have been faced with the fact of human mortality—not only in the physical or even spiritual sense, but in a moral sense as well.

And yet we must remember: I am only *thinking* about torture, while elsewhere there are actual human beings held in lightless cells, starving and frozen, undergoing electroshock, being beaten, being raped. Their suffering is not in the least abstract. Their confrontation with horror is not in any sense voluntary. Their nightmares, I would wager, are not so easily allayed.

Part Two:
Media Silence
and Public Opinion

Amerikai Modszerek: Kinzas Es Az Vralom Logikaja: Interview by Gyozo Nehez

(*Indymedia.hu*, October 22, 2006.)

Gyozo Nehez: First, tell the readers something about yourself!

Kristian Williams: I'm an anarchist living in Portland, Oregon. If you look at a map of the U.S., Oregon is all the way at the left and about 2/3 of the way to the top, just north of California. For the past ten years, I've been involved with local efforts against police brutality, most recently with an organization called Rose City Copwatch. Copwatch teaches people about their legal rights, videotapes the cops when they interact with the public, and tries to influence the debate around public safety in ways that promote non-state responses to community needs. My intellectual work grew directly out of my activism.

I've written two books about state violence. The first, *Our Enemies in Blue: Police and Power in America*, came out in 2004. . . . My second book, *American Methods: Torture and the Logic of Domination*, came out this past spring [2006]. *American Methods* deals with the U.S. government's use of torture, starting with an analysis of the Abu Ghraib scandal.

Nehez: As you write in the introduction, your book is not ultimately about Abu Ghraib in Baghdad. It is instead about torture in general and about the U.S.A. What was your aim with this book?

Williams: The American people are very confused right now. And I don't mean that in a condescending way, like if you don't agree with me then you're suffering under false consciousness or something. No, I mean that for a very large number of people, if you ask them about what is happening in the country, or with America's role in the world, they tell you that they don't understand it, that they don't know what to think about it. That's true about a lot of things—the September 11 attack, the whole war in Iraq—and I think it was particularly true about the Abu Ghraib pictures. Here were these horrible photos, which really vividly showed our soldiers behaving like monsters. And people just couldn't understand it. I wanted to help them understand why torture was occurring at Abu Ghraib, and moreover, I wanted to show them that, for very similar reasons, the same kinds of abuses continue to occur not just overseas, but in our domestic prisons as well. I wanted to provide some context for those ghastly snapshots.

Nehez: What kind of impression did the Abu Ghraib story make on the American people? To what extent is the culture of violation accepted, in view of American history?

Williams: Nearly everyone was shocked. And not merely shocked, but horrified.

There were a few right-wing pundits who tried to justify it, but they were an embarrassing fringe. More commonly, the authorities tried to minimize the significance of the events at Abu Ghraib— saying it was just a few soldiers at one base, and that it in no way reflected on the war effort, or military, as a whole. People were pretty willing to believe that, and largely just assumed that anything so terrible had to be some sort of anomaly.

Of course, the military's own investigations reached the opposite conclusion, and careful reading shows how the torture at Abu Ghraib, and similar abuses elsewhere, came as a predictable consequence of policy decisions made a couple years earlier.

In *American Methods*, I push the analysis further, and argue that the policy decisions characterizing the War on Terror fit neatly in a long historical arc of U.S. imperialism. But the sad fact is, the American public as a whole is almost completely unaware of that history.

Nehez: Has the American public connected the story of Abu Ghraib with the NSA's phone taps (without court supervision) and the Patriot Act giving the FBI the power to search people's homes without notifying them? Can they see the overall pattern in terms of repression? Think about the relationship between violation and state power. . .

Williams: Critics list those items—torture,

wiretaps, secret searches—with a lot of Bush's other misdeeds, but they rarely make any effort to explain to the public the underlying logic that connects them.

The reporting around this sort of thing is very fragmented, so that you might have separate articles in the same issue of a newspaper addressing Bush's torture policy, the NSA wiretap program, and, say, an FBI raid based on secret evidence—and yet there'd be no attempt to connect these stories to one another. They're presented as having as little to do with each other as the stock numbers and the sports section.

That's ironic, because it's easy to show how they relate. As genuinely stupid as George Bush is, the clique behind him does have something of a philosophy. In their view, power isn't just a means to achieve their agenda, it's *the central piece* of the agenda—power of the state over the citizenry, power of the President over the judiciary and the legislature, power of the U.S. over the world. What they're seeking is the Hobbesian ideal of sovereignty, with the ruler being above the law. And they want to extend this power over the entire globe. The War on Terror, in both its international and domestic aspects, is very much animated by this philosophy.

When I was writing the first draft of *American Methods*, I read Assistant Attorney General Jay Bybee's famous torture memos. In these documents he puts forward an astounding argument that, given the President's role as Commander in Chief, and given the context of the War on Terror, there are no legally valid limits to what the President can do to protect the American people: Not the Geneva Conventions, not the federal anti-torture law, not the War Crimes Act. What he advocates is a straightforward totalitarian principle, with the President as *Fuhrer*. To give some idea of what this might mean, I pointed out that in this particular memo it justifies torture, but it could also justify warrantless wiretaps, or Watergate-style black-bag jobs, or a nationwide system of military checkpoints. I came up with those examples out of my head, but by the time I was doing my revisions it had been revealed that arguments very much like Bybee's had been put forward within the administration to justify warrantless wiretapping. And shortly after the book went to press, we got some good evidence that the feds had conducted at least one black-bag job in an effort to cover up the wiretap program. It's one of those situations where you don't relish being proved right.

Nehez: What is the message of Guantánamo prisons for politicians in the rest of the world?

Williams: Guantánamo is a good example of what I'm talking about. The base was located where it is for the explicit purpose of putting it—and its prisoners—outside the law. The Bush administration argued that since it wasn't in the U.S. itself, no law applied at the prison. And at the same time the administration was saying that

prisoners captured in Afghanistan were "enemy combatants," not Prisoners of War, thus excluding them from the protections of the Geneva Conventions. If we put these arguments together, the prisoners at Guantánamo had literally no rights. Legally speaking, that was nonsense. But it did send a clear message to the rest of the world: The U.S. intends to exempt itself from international law; it acknowledges no limits to the ways it can treat its opponents.

Nehez: Ignoring of the Geneva Conventions, as well as norms of international law, is not a special feature of George W. Bush. His father was President George Herbert Walker Bush, whose invasion against Panama was a typical example of this attitude. For Central-European people it has a special importance, because the invasion of Panama and the arrest of General Noriega happened just when Eastern Europe was set free from the Soviet oppression. But we could also mention President Clinton's Secretary of State Madeline Albright's famous statement: "Multilaterally when possible, but unilaterally when necessary. . ."

Williams: Yes, the first President Bush also declared that the Geneva Conventions did not legally pertain to the invasion of Panama, though he left their provisions in place as a matter of policy. And it was Clinton who started the CIA's extraordinary rendition program, in which official enemies are kidnapped and shipped to other countries for torture. The current President Bush has merely intensified a tendency that was already well entrenched. If America ever has its version of the Nuremberg tribunals, we can look forward to seeing these three men in the dock together.

Nehez: On the day after 9/11 *Le Monde* declared, "We are all American now," but sympathy for the United States has changed into suspicion and, for some, into hatred. The prisons at Guantánamo Bay and Abu Ghraib, the treatment of prisoners, secret prisons and flights all added to this feeling. Today people outside of America want to distance themselves from American policy. . .

Williams: Plenty of people *inside* America want to distance themselves from American policy. In fact, plenty of people in the President's own party want to distance themselves from his policies!

A lot of this has to do with Iraq. The politicians seem to have suddenly remembered one of the major lessons of Vietnam: The public will sometimes forgive you for starting an unpopular and illegal war—but never for losing one.

The question is how much it matters. Bush's approval ratings are in the toilet, but the anti-war movement, by and large, is disorganized and ineffectual. Both Republican and Democratic politicians are becoming more vocal in their criticisms of Bush's policies, but it mostly smells

of election-year posturing. Despite their grousing, Republicans in Congress keep rubber-stamping Bush's proposals—and Democrats are hard pressed to say how they would do things much differently, even if they won control of both houses of Congress. Internationally the situation is pretty similar. The U.N. and the E.U. gripe about Guantánamo and the extraordinary rendition program, but as long as their member countries keep cooperating, who cares?

My sense is that the current administration is not overly concerned with public opinion, or even with keeping things smooth with their allies internationally. They've decided that it's better to be feared than loved, and so they don't really worry about criticism—they worry about resistance.

Nehez: What can people do to energize democracy now?

Williams: That's a good question. To some degree it's a chicken-and-egg problem, because the way we mobilize people is by delivering real victories, and the way we win is by creating broad-based social movements. The good news is that once the process gets going, a virtuous cycle can set in. But in the mean time it's hard to know where to start.

I can't really speak to conditions in Hungary, but in the U.S. most people feel really powerless to affect any actual change and the left has become almost resigned to its irrelevancy.

If you ask activists what purpose is served by a protest march, I think most would say something like, "to voice our opposition against the war." The connection between "voicing opposition" and *stopping* the war is left vague. Because of this, the anti-war movement has squandered some real opportunities. Millions of people demonstrated before the invasion of Iraq, but there was no real plan for how to respond when the invasion happened anyway—even though everyone knew it would. All those people felt defeated and powerless, and a lot of momentum was lost. Three years later, the movement still hasn't fully recovered. A lot of people have been left with the feeling that opposition is pointless. Our first task has to be showing them that it's not, that change is still possible.

It's been done before. The anti-globalization movement's development in the U.S. is a good recent example. When Clinton signed the North American Free Trade Agreement, the deal faced only token opposition domestically. But the left continued to press the issue of globalization, working steadily for years on anti-sweatshop campaigns and the like, building working alliances between unions, environmental organizations, and human rights groups. By 1999, there was a sizable bit of the population who not only opposed corporate globalization, but had actively participated in some aspect of the struggle against it. That November,

tens of thousands of protesters succeeded in derailing the World Trade Organization meeting in Seattle. It was an unexpected victory, and the anti-globalization movement got a huge boost—in the U.S. especially. Tons more people got involved, protests got bigger, and direct action tactics suddenly had a legitimacy that was unthinkable a year or so before. Shutting down the WTO meeting was certainly worth doing for its own sake, but the real benefit was that it wildly expanded our sense of the possible.

Nehez: Alice Walker in her book *Anything We Love Can Be Saved* writes that Malcolm X, Martin Luther King, Jr., and Rosa Parks all represent activism at its most contagious, because it is always linked to celebration and joy. . . .

Williams: Unfortunately, there isn't a lot to celebrate at our present moment. But still, isn't it interesting that that sense of joy remains attached to resistance? I think it's because resistance affirms our humanity, our dignity. It makes us more fully human. But I think that's more an outcome than a cause of struggle. At the outset, I think it's more important to have a sense of hope, that things can be different and through our actions we can contribute to that change. The joy comes later, from struggle itself as much as from victory.

Gyozo Nehez is an activist, a member of ATTAC Hungary.

Against Self-Censorship: Countering CBS's Critics

(*Extra!* August 2004.)

When General Richard Myers called CBS and asked that they delay their exposé of the Abu Ghraib prison scandal, the network complied. Now some journalists are challenging its decision to show the photos at all.

The more thoughtful objections have come from the *National Review Online*'s Jonah Goldberg, with backing from *Slate*'s Mickey Kaus. They offer three basic arguments.

1) First, there is the demand for consistency.

Goldberg writes,

"[the media] can help Americans 'appreciate' the Nick Berg beheading by showing it over and over. I don't know if that would be a good idea, but at least the press would be consistent."

Kaus invokes ethical constraints on identifying CIA agents, outing gays, or printing "grisly photos of Nicole Simpson's near-decapitated corpse."

The difference is a matter of relevance. Whereas it is rarely important to name CIA operatives, discuss the sexuality of public figures, or show crime scene photos, the images from Abu Ghraib are not simply colorful details or sensational flourishes. As Donald Rumsfeld acknowledged: "It is the photographs that gives one the vivid realization of what actually took place. Words don't do it."

This might also be true of the Berg video. But it is hard to say what we would *learn* from viewing that footage, since no one doubts that terrorists are willing to brutally murder innocent people. In contrast, before *60 Minutes II* broadcast the Abu Ghraib photos, it was contentious to claim that American soldiers were deliberately abusing Iraqi civilians. Now the questions are: How commonly does this abuse occur? And, under whose orders?

2) The second argument stresses the consequences of publishing the photos.

Goldberg writes,

"These pictures are so inflammatory, so offensive to Muslim and American sensibilities, whatever news value they have is far, far outweighed by the damage they are doing."

He cites former *Guardian* editor Peter Preston's principle that the news shouldn't get anyone killed.

By this standard, the video of Rodney King's beating should have been suppressed so as to avoid riots, and the images of the September 11 attacks ought not to have appeared on television, lest they incite hate crimes and war. Like it or not, we can't demand that the news be harmless without restricting it to trivia.

In an odd way, CBS's critics concede a point that conservatives have snickered about for the last three years—that America's behavior overseas might make us less safe. Kaus argues that:

"There is a large amorphous group of 'swing voter' Arabs who might support terrorism but who might also be persuaded to live at peace with the encroaching forces of globalization. . . . If you buy [this idea], as do many of Donald Rumsfeld's critics on the left, and as do I, then you really didn't want these photos published, because they are what will lose us the swing voters and produce the blowback. . . ."

This ingenious inversion of the liberal argument shifts blame from the military to the press. By this thinking, it is not the army's atrocities that create resentment abroad, but the media's coverage of those atrocities.

Goldberg concurs:

"The Iraqi insurgents had to have known that there were abuses taking place in Abu Ghraib before these images were released. . .

. [But] the revelation of those humiliating pictures and the political opportunities they created lead to Berg's beheading."

The argument is less sophisticated than it sounds: Goldberg begins by assuming that "the release of the photos—and not the abuse" prompted Berg's murder, and then concludes that the media rather than the military is to blame for the killing. But is there any reason to believe that without the pictures al-Qaeda's allies would have let Berg live?

Even on strictly utilitarian grounds, these arguments are weak. We can't just *assume* that the negative consequences outweigh the positive. Sure, there is the murder of Nicholas Berg to consider. But there is also the mass release of prisoners—most of them innocent, according to military sources. There is the public scrutiny of the military's interrogation practices. And there is a wave of national soul-searching that has the potential to prevent similar abuses and might make our country less eager to wage war. Earlier reports of abuse failed to produce these good results, arguably because they lacked the photographs.

3) The critics' third argument concerns the media's obligations during wartime.

"I wouldn't publish the sailing dates of troop ships," Kaus writes. "The Abu Ghraib photo situation is very close to that one. . . ."

It is? Unlike information on troop movements, details of prisoner abuse are not of any military use to America's opponents. The photos reveal war crimes, not battle plans. They do not involve legitimate military activities and so they cannot be treated as legitimate military secrets.

The photos are dangerous, but for political—not military—reasons. This is the difference between dissent and treason. Confusion on this point stifles criticism of the government during wartime, and Goldberg actively conflates the two aspects of the conflict:

"The Abu Ghraib images are so shocking, so offensive, and so sensational they will in all likelihood make America's job in Iraq and the Middle East immeasurably harder for a long time to come. That means more American deaths—such as Berg's—more Iraqi deaths and a diminished future for that country and that region."

The remarkable thing about this argument—all these arguments, really—is the ideological commitment to America's imperial project. Goldberg opposes the publication of images that might make "America's job in Iraq" harder. Kaus is worried about the effect on "'swing voter' Arabs" and their willingness to accept "the encroaching forces of globalization." Interestingly, neither talk about how the scandal might affect American attitudes.

They assume the legitimacy of America's geopolitical position, and advance accordingly. But there are good reasons to doubt the beneficence of our country's global hegemony. Some of these reasons are vividly illustrated in the photographs from Abu Ghraib. That is why the pictures are dangerous. And that is why the public needs to see them.

Keeping the State's Secrets

(*The World Today*, February 2006.)

All the news that's fit to print, indeed.

In December [2005], the *New York Times* revealed a top-secret National Security Agency program to tap American phones without court approval. The story triggered what is probably the most intense political crisis of President George Bush's administration, with at least one judge resigning in protest, senators pushing for official hearings, and even conservative commentators acknowledging possible grounds for impeachment. The only thing Bush has to be thankful about is that the story did not break during his re-election campaign.

And so the *Times* did the President a favor, since the paper seems to have known about the phone-tapping program before the November 2004 vote and kept it quiet at the administration's request.

The December 16 article offered little by way of explanation:

"The White House asked the *New York Times* not to publish this article, arguing that it could jeopardize continuing investigations and alert would-be terrorists that they might be under scrutiny. After meeting senior administration officials to hear their concerns, the newspaper delayed publication for a year to conduct additional reporting. Some information that administration officials argued could be useful to terrorists has been omitted."

Criticisms have come at the paper hard and fast, from left and right. The left complains that the story did not run sooner; the right wishes it had never seen ink. Criticism even came from the paper's own ranks. Anonymous *New York Times* employees have told their colleagues at the *New York Observer* and the *Los Angeles Times* that the journalists were pushing for earlier publication, hoping to bring out the story before the election.

When the editors sank it, reporter James Risen took a year off to write his book *State of War*—released just after the article appeared. As one source inside the paper told the *Los Angeles Times*, the forthcoming book changed the equation:

"When they realized that [the NSA story] was going to appear in the book anyway, that is when they went ahead and agreed to publish the story. . . . That's not to say that was their entire consideration, but it was a very important one."

In the January 1 paper, Byron Calame, the *New York Times*' public editor, admitted that he did not really know what to make of the paper's stalling, or its "woefully inadequate" explanations—

in part because other editors blocked his inquiries. Calame outlined his own cautious worries. He noted that the paper's original explanation seemed to imply that "the article was fully confirmed and ready to publish a year ago—after perhaps weeks of reporting on the initial tip." And, he added that the decision to publish now was somewhat suspect, since "the paper was quite aware that it faced the possibility of being scooped by its own reporter's book in about four weeks."

Bill Keller, the *Times'* executive editor, insists that neither the election nor Risen's book were ever factors. He released a statement explaining, instead:

> "the Administration argued strongly that writing about this eavesdropping program would give terrorists clues about the vulnerability of their communications and would deprive the government of an effective tool for the protection of the country's security. Officials also assured senior editors of the *Times* that a variety of legal checks had been imposed that satisfied everyone involved that the program raised no legal questions."

But after a year of further investigations, Keller says, the *Times* learned that agents within the NSA questioned the program's legality, and the editors determined that it would be possible to write the story without exposing any specific intelligence methods.

In other words, the editor's official position is that he was suckered. He was too willing to believe the government's dire warnings about what would happen if the policy was undermined, and ready to accept the warm assurances about the program's lawfulness. Such gullibility is a major shortcoming for a journalist under any circumstances, but in this case it is particularly unforgivable.

Given the Bush administration's long record of less-than-truthful pronouncements and its sprawling interpretation of presidential powers, only a fool would trust the White House's judgment about the legality, or the necessity, of a vast, secret spying program—especially when the revelations of the program would, at the very least, cause the President a great deal of political embarrassment and could potentially cost him the election.

Think for a minute about the fabricated justifications for war in Iraq and the legal gymnastics of the 2002 Justice Department torture memos, and ask yourself whether a newspaper editor should take Bush's word for anything. If the President told me the sky was blue, I'd be sure to look outside before I put it in the paper.

Whatever the editors' motives, the decision spared the President an election-year scandal and allowed the government to escape scrutiny for a deliberate violation of the Foreign

Intelligence Surveillance Act. It is hard to think of a clearer case of a newspaper neglecting its responsibility to the public interest.

Still, the *Times* unfortunately has plenty of company in its willingness to acquiesce. On November 2, 2005, the *Washington Post* revealed that the Central Intelligence Agency was running a system of secret prisons around the world, including jails in "several democracies in Eastern Europe." The *Post* explained that it deliberately avoided

> "publishing the names of the Eastern European countries involved in the covert program, at the request of senior U.S. officials. They argued that the disclosure might disrupt counterterrorism efforts in those countries and elsewhere and could make them targets of possible terrorist retaliation."

In a National Public Radio interview the day the article appeared, its author, Dana Priest, offered a very important variation to the official line:

> "senior officials did ask us not to publish the names of the countries. . . . They made an argument . . . that *it could lead to possible disruption of counterterrorists' cooperation with these countries* and possible terrorist retaliations" (emphasis added).

The *Post* uses the misleadingly neutral rhetoric of national security to dress up political concerns—specifically, the willingness of European democracies to continue playing the Bush game when faced with public opposition, and the possibility that these same countries would make some unpleasant enemies if their role was known.

Perhaps the Bush administration did seek to shield its allies from terrorist threats. Undoubtedly it was concerned about the disruption of its activities and hoped to avoid a repeat of its experience in Thailand: When it was revealed that the U.S. was operating a secret prison there, public outrage and international pressure forced the Thai government to close it.

Worse, the *Post* seems to have compromised its scoop for practically no benefit. Really, the only new information in the article was, paradoxically, the same information the *Post* refused to detail. It had been known for some time that the CIA was running a covert prison system, just not that it had detention facilities in Europe. By withholding the precise locations, the paper missed an opportunity for genuine revelation.

Luckily, Human Rights Watch was not so squeamish. Within a week it had identified Mihail Kogalniceanu, Romania and Szczytno, Poland as likely "black sites." The governments there deny it, but the controversy has persisted, prompting an EU investigation and greatly souring Condoleezza Rice's European tour.

Something similar happened with the Abu Ghraib torture scandal. CBS's *60 Minutes II* sat on the infamous photographs for two weeks at the request of General Richard B. Myers. Dan Rather justified the decision by citing "the danger and tension on the ground in Iraq."

Apparently, Myers had argued for the delay based on the photographs' potential to inflame Iraqi anger at a time when marines were putting down the uprising in Fallujah and insurgents were keeping several Americans hostage. Myers specifically warned that publication of the photos would "kill Americans."

In April 2004, CBS pushed ahead with the story, in order to outrace the *New Yorker's* publication of the photographs and an accompanying article by Seymour Hersh—who apparently never considered holding back the story.

When the Abu Ghraib story broke, there was minor grousing from the *National Review*, but the results were undeniably good. The Abu Ghraib photos did for torture what the Rodney King video did for police brutality—moved it from the back pages to the front, and shifted it in the public mind from paranoid rumor to verified fact. More than that, it led to the release of hundreds of prisoners, encouraged media attention to U.S. human rights abuses elsewhere,

emboldened other whistle-blowers, and provided some of the motivation behind Senator John McCain's anti-torture bill. In fact, it is hard to know whether the subsequent scandals—those concerning secret prisons and NSA wiretaps—would have found their traction without the unsettling precedent of Abu Ghraib.

In each of these cases, the story did come out. But the willingness of the media to stall publication—whether for the sake of national security or the convenience of politicians—is worrying. What other stories are being delayed, or buried permanently, for similar reasons?

What's most embarrassing, and most troubling, is how little pressure it takes to win the media's silence. None of the journalists, editors, or publishers involved allege official efforts to censor the stories, or harm their careers through McCarthy-style blackmail and blacklisting. Nor do they cite worries about lawsuits, prison sentences, or physical violence—though, to be fair, reporters could face jail when the Justice Department asks them to identify their sources. Instead, they cite "requests" from the administration and concerns about "national security"—as though it were the media's job to keep the government's secrets, even when that means hiding official crimes.

Part Three:
Torture, Democracy, and Inequality

Prisons, Torture, & Imperialism: Interview by David Cunningham

(Anti-Poverty Committee Prison Justice Journal, Winter 2006.)

David Cunningham: What are the relationships between torture in prisons and imperialism?

Kristian Williams: Part of my argument in *American Methods* is that we can't only look at torture as it's used by the military overseas, or as it's used in prisons at home. If we do, not only do we get an incomplete picture, but a distorted one. To understand the U.S. government's use of torture we have to look at both aspects.

It's not just that the photos from Abu Ghraib *look* similar to abuses in America's prisons at home. There's a transfer of tactics, technology, personnel, and organizational models between these two institutions: Charles Graner and Ivan Frederick, two of the ringleaders among the Abu Ghraib guards, were prison guards in the U.S. before going to Iraq. Military Police in Iraq and Afghanistan were trained in "pain compliance" techniques by guards working in domestic prisons. The isolation cells at Guantánamo were modeled on the Secure Housing Units and super-maximum security prisons operating in the U.S.—which is why no one should be surprised at the psychological distress,

self-harm, and suicides in Gitmo; we've seen the same thing happen to prisoners in long-term isolation in U.S. prisons.

A lot of the bloodiest assaults in Guantánamo came at the hands of the Internal Reaction Force—or as the inmates call it, the "Extreme Reaction Force." They are a squad in riot gear that handles disturbances and forces recalcitrant inmates out of their cells during searches. The ERF was modeled on similar units in U.S. prisons, which were modeled on SWAT teams in U.S. police departments. SWAT teams—as their creator, former L.A. Police Chief Daryl Gates, likes to brag—were modeled on Special Forces units in the U.S. military. So we have the whole circuit—from military, to police, to prison, to military prison. And I'm sure later we'll hear about innovations from Gitmo being circulated back again to domestic agencies.

That's on the practical level. Politically speaking, the use of torture domestically is related to imperialism because they promote the same agenda. They serve the same interests, and bolster the power of the state at the expense of individual rights.

It's typical in the U.S. to talk about foreign policy and domestic policy as though the two really don't have anything to do with each other. But it's the same government. And the same people, more or less, set the agenda in each area. Prisons, police, and the U.S. Marines all defend the existing distribution of power; they defend a system in which poor people, people of color, and women are systematically disadvantaged for the benefit of a relatively few wealthy white people.

This parallel is reflected in the strategic orientation of the various institutions as well. I argued in my first book, *Our Enemies in Blue*, that policing in the U.S. now operates along the lines of a counter-insurgency program—a direct example of imperial power infecting domestic relations.

Cunningham: How does the use of torture in prisons affect the state's uses of social control on its general population?

Williams: It's a terrorist enterprise. Torture works, not only to coerce its most immediate victims, but also to intimidate those who hear of it. During the "dirty wars" in Latin America, the process of "disappearance" didn't just silence people who were kidnapped and murdered, it also silenced others like them. It wasn't only guerrillas or their supporters who were targeted, it was also journalists, teachers, lawyers, human rights advocates, and sometimes their friends and relatives. The effect of that sort of campaign was broadly felt and the political culture in places like Chile still hasn't completely recovered.

Things in the U.S. today look quite a lot different, but the principle is pretty much the same. Police brutality, racial profiling, and mass incarceration together reinforce the existing system of racial inequality and—especially during the past three decades of prison expansion—have had a devastating effect on the Black community. Prison has become a constantly looming presence, casting a shadow over the lives of select portions of the population. And the threat of prison carries the threat of torture and, in particular, rape.

This threat is more present for some of us than others. Black men are almost seven times more likely to be jailed than white men. Immigrants are increasingly facing detention, often in conditions as bad as those in criminal jails. And of course poor people of all races fill the cells at a much higher rate than the wealthy corporate crooks.

Prison doesn't just reflect the power imbalances in society at large, it's also a means by which they are reproduced. Ex-cons have difficulty finding work and housing. In many states, they are barred from voting. And those on probation or parole are shouldered with impossibly detailed rules and allowed almost no rights, while enduring the constant threat of being literally caged. That's just one way that prison—and therefore, torture—underwrites the state's authority overall and grounds a great deal of the system of social control.

It's important to keep this in mind as we struggle to end torture. It's not enough to prohibit the abusive practices or to try to enforce existing human rights law—though that is important. We also have to change the underlying social conditions that make torture profitable for those who use it. That means reducing the power of the state's coercive apparatus, both domestically and in warfare. It means correcting the fundamental social inequalities—especially those based on race, class, and gender.

David Cunningham is a member of the Anti-Poverty Committee in Vancouver, British Columbia.

Hidden Torture, False Democracy:
a review of *Torture and Democracy*, by Darius Rejali (Princeton University Press, 2007).

(*International Socialist Review*, September-October 2008.)

Darius Rejali's *Torture and Democracy* represents a profound achievement. It explains how torture has changed over the last century, especially in the last thirty-five years. It describes the developments in technique and traces their transfer from one place to another, documenting what methods were used when, where, and by whom. The techniques are listed, described, classified, and carefully placed within a broader historical context. Anyone wanting to understand waterboarding, or forced standing, or the differences between electro-torture and shock therapy, can find the answers they're looking for here. *Torture and Democracy* is, in fact, exactly the resource I wished I'd had when I was researching my own book on torture, *American Methods*.

Rejali's contribution to the field is substantial, and *Torture and Democracy* is likely the most important book on the subject to be published in the last twenty years. But it is disappointing, for just that reason: it's inadequate in dealing with the *politics* of torture.

To be clear, let me say again that Rejali's research is solid, his writing is crisp, his thinking is original, and the history he outlines marks a serious step forward in our understanding of the state's cruelest practices. But his unexamined assumptions—especially about the nature of democracy—cripple his analysis and greatly limit the usefulness of his book.

Three Books In One

No one would describe *Torture and Democracy* as an easy read. The text alone is 551 pages, with another 38 pages for four appendices, and 225 pages of notes and bibliographic material. And then there's the subject matter.

Only devoted scholars are going to read it all the way through, but the book is more accessible than one might expect. The prose is lucid and the social science jargon is kept to a minimum. The major stylistic flaws—repetition and interminable-seeming lists of torture techniques—are probably unavoidable given the length, scope, and nature of the book.

Rejali set out to accomplish several goals at once:

"(1) to offer a history of the technology of torture around the globe over the past century and use it to engage historical, philosophical, and anthropological claims about modern torture,

(2) to raise provocative questions and hypotheses about the historical

pattern of torture technology and the factors that shape it, relating the development of this technology to elements not normally considered connected to it, namely, democracy and international monitoring,
(3) to change public debate,
(4) to offer a riposte to those who defend the use of torture, and
(5) to provide a reliable sourcebook for human-rights organizations, policymakers, and politicians, drawing extensively on sources hitherto unavailable in English or so scattered and obscure as to be almost inaccessible."
(Paragraph breaks added for clarity.)

Rejali meets some of these quite well, but it's not always clear what his multiple goals really have to do with each other, or what each of his various audiences are supposed to make of all the material that is essentially superfluous for their respective purposes.

Many of the chapters work as stand-alone pieces, so it's often possible to find the information you need already organized in a chapter-length package reasonably independent of the surrounding material. Chapter 10, for example, offers a thorough—and surprisingly fascinating—history of taser and stun-gun technology. Anyone interested in taking these pernicious weapons away from their local police would do well to familiarize themselves with this material. It's a much

smaller group that will need to read the entire 136 pages of "A History of Electric Stealth"—though the full story is probably the most interesting, and certainly the most developed, of the several technical histories contained in the book.

I repeatedly found myself wishing that Rejali had written three short books instead of one long one. The history of electro-torture would be one of these. Another would cover the broader history of torture in the twentieth century, explaining the turn toward stealthy techniques, while the third would take on the arguments that justify the use of torture.

Ethics and Efficacy

The third of these books would address the questions that lay people find most pressing—and would contain what I consider to be the book's best section, comprising chapters titled, "Does Torture Work?," "What the Apologists Say," "Why Governments Don't Learn," and "The Great Age of Torture in Modern Memory." For this reason, I'd suggest readers consider starting with this section, and then engage the earlier chapters with its arguments in mind.

"Does Torture Work?" reviews the empirical evidence on the efficacy of torture to retrieve accurate information. Rejali concludes that, given its abysmal record and the ineradicable problems inherent to the use of torture, *anything* would be a better means for collecting intelligence—flipping coins, reading tea leaves, shooting randomly into crowds, or doing nothing at all. "What the Apologists Say" then goes after the claims of torture enthusiasts, most famously the attorney Alan Dershowitz. "Why Governments Don't Learn" considers the possibilities for regulating torture and argues that torture is inherently resistant to such regulation. The final chapter, "The Great Age of Torture in Modern Memory," examines the ways we remember, misremember, and fictionalize the history of torture— and the implications of these stories that we tell ourselves.

These four chapters would nicely complement Henry Shue's essay, "Torture," which first appeared in *Philosophy and Public Affairs* in 1978. Shue's approach is mainly theoretical. He articulates the ethical problems with torture and exposes the logical flaws in arguments intended to justify its use— specifically by identifying the suppressed assumptions of ticking-bomb cases. Shue writes:

"hard cases make bad law, and . . . artificial cases make bad ethics. . . . [O]ne cannot easily draw conclusions for ordinary cases from extraordinary ones, and as the situations described [by apologists] become more likely, the conclusion that the torture is permissible becomes more debatable. . . . The distance between the situations which must be concocted in order to have a plausible case of morally permissible torture and the situations which actually occur is, if anything, further reason why the existing prohibitions against torture should remain."

Rejali argues along similar lines, but rather than emphasize the in-principle limits of imaginary cases, he goes a step further, forcing the debate onto the terrain of hard reality. He writes:

"Apologists often assume that torture works, and all that is left is the moral justification. If torture does not work, then their apology is irrelevant."

He then looks carefully at the historical record and uses the facts of the apologists' own favorite stories—the Battle of Algiers, in particular—to systematically debunk their rationalizations. He concludes:

"whenever apologists claim empirical insight, everyone should simply ask them repeatedly for the evidence, check the sources, and double-check the claim with other sources. Nothing apologists have advanced so far has withstood the light of day."

Between these two attacks, there is no room in which to wedge a justifying pretext. In a sense, Rejali has completed the philosophical project that

Shue began thirty years ago. That alone would be enough to qualify *Torture and Democracy* as an invaluable contribution to the debate.

Civilization and Masculinity

So if torture fails so badly, why do Dershowitz-style intellectuals continue to defend it? And why is the public drawn to such arguments?

In the final pages of *Torture and Democracy*, Rejali suggests that a major cultural and psychological motivator in the acceptance of torture is our conception of masculinity. Individually, the torturer feels the need to prove that he is tough and decisive, that he is in control and will do whatever needs to be done. Collectively, torture is intended to remedy "a long-felt, common anxiety that democracy has made us weak and there are no real men anymore." We identify torture with strength, democracy with weakness.

It's an interesting idea, one that a lot of people—myself included—have struggled to articulate and mostly come up short. Rejali's treatment of this debate in *Torture and Democracy* is too brief, but he discusses it more fully in his 2007 article from the *South Central Review*, "Torture Makes the Man." That essay relates, with striking eloquence, the drive to torture with deeply rooted Western conceptions of manliness, racial superiority, and imperial messianism. Drawing from sources as varied as Leopold von Sacher-Masoch's *Venus in Furs*, Frantz Fanon's *Black Skins, White Masks* and *The Wretched of the Earth*, Jean Lartéguy's *The Centurions*, and John Noyes's *The Mastery of Submission*, the essay manages to relate racialized fears of sexual licentiousness, the modern dread of the primitive and the natural, warrior ideals of masculinity—and the masculine idealization of war—and the eroticization of suffering and of power.

Rejali writes in his essay:

"[W]ould you torture a terrorist if you knew he had planted a bomb and hundreds of innocents were going to die? . . . Either you do so, and prove you're a man. Or you do not, and then you show you are weak, because your values—democratic, enlightened, liberal, idealistic—made you weak. . . .

The conception of masculinity that informs the judgment, 'Yes, I would torture,' is based on deep doubts about the life one is living, about the values one is allegedly defending through torture, and ultimately, about one's own masculinity. . . .

Those who do not think we can win by means of these [democratic] principles harbor deep doubts, not about the strength of al-Qaeda, but about the founding beliefs of our civilization. They worry that we have become sissies and our enemies know it. Nothing will shake their belief in torture's efficacy, no matter how much evidence is provided, because this belief is so wrapped up with their perception of themselves."

The article is sweeping in its analysis, and radical in its implications. Torture, by this reading, remains a sort of blood sacrifice intended to settle our unease about the nature of our civilization. We find comfort in torture, because we fear equality.

"[T]he terrorist's suffering is uniquely satisfying regardless of whether he reveals any information. Beneath the urbane, civilized appeal to torture for information, lurks a deeper impulse, born of fear and satisfied by pain. . . . [I]t is difficult to understand why this response (as opposed to so many others) is so satisfying without acknowledging that [through torture] officials are also purging the wounded community's furious emotions with human sacrifices. . . . Strategic talk about torture in the face of terrorism turns out to have a deep undercurrent of blood lust."

If this is right, then torture does not only function as a means of intimidation and public terror, but also symbolically creates a sphere of perceived protection and inclusion. By identifying the enemy with its actual or potential victims, torture also implicitly constructs a public—an "imagined community"—that its practices purport to keep safe. When people identify themselves with the privileged, protected "us" and not the tortured, terrorized "them," the result will enhance both their sense of in-group solidarity and belonging, and their direct loyalty to the state. This effect is most easily produced when "we" and "they" are also divided along identifiable lines of race, ethnicity, or religion.

These ideological factors do not simply *cause* the state's violence, but they do help to legitimize it. The state's relationship to torture is chiefly instrumental, but the cultural backdrop undoubtedly helps to shape its specific practices, motivate its individual functionaries (both at the policy and the tactical levels), set the terms of debate, and maintain a deep ambivalence in public opinion.

Interrogating Democracy

Unfortunately, this compelling deconstruction of the rationales for torture and the curious history of electrical torture are in a way incidental to the central project of the book—demonstrating that it was the democracies, and not authoritarian governments, that introduced the main innovations in torture during the twentieth century. It's here that Rejali really gets himself into trouble. The research is as thorough, and the writing is as graceful, but the politics are thin—and the failure to challenge some basic liberal assumptions confuses the analysis and presentation.

Rejali's main thesis, as he provocatively presents it early on, is that "clean torture and democracy go hand in hand." *Clean* torture, here, is in contradistinction to *scarring* torture; and *democracy* is contrasted with *authoritarian* government. The first of these distinctions is astute; the second is confused.

"Clean methods" include sleep deprivation, electro-shock, certain types of beatings, suffocation and partial drowning, forced standing and exhaustion exercises, and the use of some drugs. Tracing the history of these and other related techniques, Rejali argues that most originated with military punishments or with slavery, found their way into the interrogation practices of "the main Western democracies" (Britain, France, and the United States), and—after a period of refinement and transference—were adopted by authoritarian states. The problem is the uncritical acceptance of the self-description of three imperial powers as "democracies."

Rejali defines the term:

"Democracy is a form of government based on amateurism (citizens rule in turn by means of lots or elections in a free choice among competitors) and participation (a significant segment of the society has access to these means). In authoritarian states, by contrast, leaders are self-appointed, or if they were elected, impossible to displace afterward. These leaders typically justify their rule by some claim other than amateurism, most commonly bureaucratic or military expertise, moral and religious authority, or their unique personal qualities such as character or descent. While some authoritarian leaders may allow participation in various national referenda, those electoral processes are highly constrained or the outcomes predetermined."

He presents this as a strict dichotomy, but the states with which he is chiefly concerned exhibit features from both categories. In the United States, for example, it is true that a "significant segment of the society" participates in a political process by which "citizens rule" via elections. But these elections are contests among elites. It is hard to reconcile the idea of "amateurism" with our apparatus of professional politicians, campaign managers, policy advisers, media consultants, and party operatives. The "citizens [who] rule" are small in number and chosen from a distinct class; and the "significant segment" that chooses them is itself a minority. Even leaving aside the systematic disenfranchisement of non-naturalized immigrants, the homeless, prisoners (and in many places, former prisoners), adolescents, and children—and ignoring for the moment the tendency of such legal exclusions to disproportionately affect the poor and people of color—it is still a minority of those eligible who engage the relatively feeble mechanism of the ballot once every few years. It is an even smaller minority that controls what appears on that ballot, and that has the dominant influence over leaders once they are elected. In this sense, our electoral processes *are* highly constrained even if the outcomes are not precisely predetermined.

This is true in another way as well: The most important issues never come up for a vote, do not feature prominently in any major debate, and are in effect ruled out in advance from honest consideration. No serious candidate for national office genuinely advocates an end to U.S. imperialism, or the nationalization of industry, or the wholesale closing of the nation's prisons. The overall structure of our society and the nature of the institutions that animate it are simply not up for discussion. Electoral debates, instead, focus inordinately on various sorts of "expertise" (usually presented in terms of "experience"), on "moral and [indirectly] religious authority," and most clearly, on matters of "character."

And when you look carefully at the nature of the main social institutions, the paucity of our "democracy" becomes apparent. Yes, we vote for Presidents and members of Congress. But we do not vote for the administrators and the generals who interpret and manage their policies; and we certainly don't vote for the low-level functionaries—the civil servants, soldiers, and police—who actually do the work of these institutions. These people "justify their rule . . . [in terms of] bureaucratic or military expertise," and from the position of the citizens they are typically "impossible to displace." No matter who we vote for, the bureaucrats remain.

Things are even worse if we turn our attention away from the state *per se* and consider society as a whole—especially if we consider the role of the private tyrannies called corporations. These are some of the most powerful institutions in our society, and they exercise enormous influence over the political system, the media, and the economy—not to mention our daily lives. But the public does not vote for them and cannot displace them. And there is no democracy in the workplace.

All this suggests that Rejali's authoritarian/democratic split is, at the very most, a continuum rather than a strict dichotomy. The study of torture offers one indication of where a society falls along that continuum—revealing both the extent of its authoritarianism and the limits of its democracy. To understand the use of torture in such systems, we should look at who is tortured, and ask who allows the torture and who benefits from it. In places, Rejali comes close to this approach.

He writes, for example:

"Police torture immigrants, the homeless, and the poor, reminding them where they can and cannot go. Torture is not the only way to generate highly segmented city streets, divide up public spaces, and create semiprivate ones (gated communities and malls). But where such demands exist, torture is not too far away."

But on the whole, *Torture and Democracy* neglects questions of inequality; it avoids addressing the real question of democracy.

"Democracy" and "authoritarianism" feature prominently as *types of states*, but appear only as formal categories nearly devoid of normative content. The difference between them comes down to a procedural question over how leaders are chosen, and there are no further criteria concerning rights and liberties, the rule of law, or legal—not to mention social—equality. In fact, Rejali explicitly excludes consideration of such values:

"Of course, someone may believe that all institutions in a democratic society should embody democratic principles.... But let us also concede that this is not an empirical position, but a normative one presented as an empirical objection. On this view, there are no democracies today and there never have been. I have no

difficulty with advancing normative ideals of democracy, but I do worry when they blind one to the ways in which torture is integrated into existing democratic societies. Then they become excuses for not dealing with the real world."

This "empirical," "real world" approach to democracy makes it possible to examine the social conditions that give rise to torture, and the uses to which torture is put, without noting the peculiarly *undemocratic* implications of those conditions, the resulting practices, or their evident aims:

"Stealthy torture . . . commonly appeared in democracies engaged in ongoing guerrilla wars, in societies that had just transitioned from authoritarian to democratic government, and in consolidated democracies with sharp civic divisions based on class or ethnicity. This corresponds to the typical conditions in which democracies turn to torture: to gather information in national security contexts, to induce false confessions, and to intimidate others and ensure civic discipline. . . ."

I take it that Rejali means to be challenging the self-presentation of governments like those of Britain, France, and the United States, deflating their opportunistic posturing on human rights. But he does so in such a way that he continuously reinforces the mythology of the "liberal democratic government."

He does this by artificially distinguishing between *democratic* and *authoritarian* regimes (even as their practices come to resemble each other's), by repeatedly identifying "public monitoring of human rights [as] a core value of democracies" (even while the governments in question develop tactics to evade monitoring), by presupposing that democracies are more responsive to public disapproval (despite the fact that authoritarian states also adopted clean methods in response to monitoring), by refusing to recognize the torture inherent in other, legal uses of the same techniques he condemns (the use of fire hoses against civil rights demonstrators, for example; or the use of pepper spray and tasers for "compliance" purposes), and by consistently failing to note the thoroughly undemocratic nature of the institutions employing torture.

Rejali's account does, certainly, reveal the stark hypocrisy of the states in question. It makes it impossible to believe simple-minded fables in which "we" are always "the good guys." But he fails to draw any substantive conclusion from these governments' failure to meet democratic norms. Either the U.S., U.K., and France fall far short of the minimum standards of democracy, in which case

democratic ideals are valid and yet there are no practicing democracies; or, "democracy" is just a word that we use in empirical studies to refer to whatever it is that countries with elected representatives actually do, in which case the ideal is an empty one and it makes no sense to try measuring by its standards.

Rejali wavers on this point, but it is the main question his work poses: *Can democracies torture?* The answer depends importantly on what we mean by "democracy"—whether we conceive of it normatively or nominally. The underlying question is whether democracy means anything more than campaign speeches and touch-screen voting—whether it *can* mean anything when these procedural devices are combined with secret prisons, indefinite detention, and water-boarding.

The Genealogy of Torture

It turns out, though, that the question of *democracy* does not affect Rejali's argument at all. Perhaps this is what allows him such complacency about the use of the word. Rejali's argument is only tangentially about democracy; what it is really about is *monitoring*.

"Why do clean torture and democracy go hand and hand? My explanation is this: public monitoring leads institutions that favor painful coercion to use and combine clean torture techniques. These methods make it less likely that torturers will be found out or held responsible. To the extent that public monitoring is not only greater in democracies, but that public monitoring of human rights is a core value in modern democracies, it is the case that where we find democracies torturing today, we will also be more likely to find police and military using multiple clean techniques."

The history he details is one in which clean tortures first arose in contexts where it was important to preserve the physical integrity of the victim—scarred slaves were harder to sell; debilitated sailors were no good aboard a ship—but in which the authorities still employed physical pain as a means of discipline. Over the course of the twentieth century, states increasingly used these techniques in warfare, in their colonies, and to control their own citizens. The first to do so were the so-called "major democracies"—Britain, France, and the United States—countries with independent media to expose abuse and judicial review of executive practices. After the Second World War, and especially since the seventies, authoritarian states—those lacking even a nominally free press or independent judiciary—also increasingly relied on clean torture practices. Rejali explains this—convincingly, I think—by pointing to the rise of international human rights monitoring and the diplomatic,

economic, and other costs associated with a bad reputation.

Rejali makes this case again and again by meticulously detailing the evolution and migration of several clean torture tactics—including many we've seen surface (again) in the present War on Terror: forced standing, sleep deprivation, clean beating, water-boarding. The story is never precisely the same for any two methods, and there are variations of period and region—but for each case, the overall pattern holds.

Yet the crucial factor, again, is not democracy, but monitoring. By Rejali's argument, both democratic and authoritarian states torture, and both seek to avoid detection when faced with independent monitoring. In short, when subject to the same pressures, they react in identical ways. The difference is that democratic states were subject to those pressures somewhat earlier than were authoritarian states. Therefore, what's really at stake is not the distinction between democratic and authoritarian states, but the tension between the state *per se* and what some have (rather optimistically) called "the new second superpower"—global civil society. It's not the type of state, but this balance of power—whether in the domestic or international sphere—that really matters.

This conclusion follows directly from Rejali's own argument. But instead of challenging leading Western governments,

Rejali continually reinforces their claims to legitimacy by focusing on the correlation between regime type and monitoring. By doing so, he suppresses any claims about the nature of real democracy.

Technical Limitations

Broadly speaking, Rejali's problem is an overemphasis on the technical at the expense of the political.

For example, he uses his mapping of specific tactics to discredit what he calls "the Universal Distributor hypothesis." This is the story, advanced by Noam Chomsky and Edward Herman, among others, that U.S. imperialism has been the driving force behind the spread of torture over the last half-century. Rejali contradicts this account by pointing to the differences in technique between U.S.-style torture and the methods of its allies in Latin America.

But this counter-claim really misses the larger point. There is plenty of evidence—much of it included in *Torture and Democracy* (see pages 427–30, for example)—that the U.S. government has trained armies in Latin America in the use of torture; Rejali merely suggests that this training was not ultimately decisive in terms of the practices they chose to employ. But this objection assumes too tight a link between the immediate causes of torture and political or moral responsibility.

It is not that important whether the U.S. government acted as the Johnny Appleseed of electro-torture in precisely the way its critics have alleged. What matters is whether or not the U.S. government knowingly allowed or encouraged its allies and client states to use torture; we might also want to ask if those friendly regimes used torture in the pursuit of aims set out by American planners or identified locally as serving U.S. interests.

The evidence is unequivocal: Yes, the U.S. government *did* knowingly allow and deliberately encourage its allies to behave in these ways, and the allies *did* use torture at least in part to serve American ends, sometimes to meet goals explicitly set out by the United States. What difference does it make, then, whether they generated the electrical current using a field telephone or some other device?

Rejali is careful not to jump to hasty conclusions; but his methodological approach may have prevented him from asking the right questions. He obsesses over the details of technique largely because he is interested in the drive behind *innovation* in torture practices, especially the turn toward clean torture. And his thesis—that the major innovations of the twentieth century came from the U.S., U.K., and France—is couched in terms of "the major democracies" (rather than, say, "the major Western imperial powers") in part because he wants to use it to defeat the more popular stories as to where these techniques came from—that is, "The Nazis did it," and "The Commies did it."

But how important are such origin stories? Why does it matter who invented water-boarding (the Dutch), given that our government is doing it *now*? Rejali's approach has something of the feel of a family history, mixed with an anxiety over original sin. Less time could be spent, I think, worrying over where these techniques come from and more given to the purposes they serve today.

Open Secrets, Selective Violence, and Social Control

Rejali understands that state violence works to maintain inequality—to keep people in line, to deter resistance, and to maintain the distance between elites and the disenfranchised. He specifically suggests that police forces use torture to maintain a public boundary between the privileged sectors of society and those who remain marginal. This view also speaks to the question of identity, to anxieties over inclusion, and ultimately, to the nature of our society. Consider:

"Who is working legally and who illegally? Who deserves the welfare of the state, and who is a vagrant who abuses it? Who benefits from legal protection, and who deserves no legal protection? How one treats citizens, guest workers, vagrants,

immigrants, and the homeless causes great controversy. Torture responds to this anxiety. . . . It works on the inside, leaving traces on habits and dispositions. Different kinds of people know where to go and where not to go, where is venturing too far and where is home. . . . Whether one can go here or there without fear of being beaten, whether one can travel in one's car without being pulled over or electrified, these are experiences constitutive of citizenship. . . . Our societies offer many finely graded distinctions between citizens, and some citizens soon discover they are not treated equally. These different civic experiences create different expectations and shape future behaviors. . . . In these cases, torture . . . is conferring identities, shaping a finely graded civic order. It reminds lesser citizens who they are and where they belong."

And yet Rejali seems ambivalent about *how* torture accomplishes these goals: He contrasts "Classical torturers [who] . . . branded or scarred in public, using bodies to advertise state power" with "modern torturers [who] favor pains, physical or psychological, that intimidate the prisoner alone."

But this cannot be right. If we assume that the only audience for torture is the immediate victim, then it could not fulfill the social function that

Rejali assigns it, marking off areas of privilege, conferring social identities, and preserving inequality. Furthermore, many of the practices of modern torture would become incomprehensible. Prison guards torture non-compliant inmates, in part to make examples out of them. Death squads go to grotesque lengths to ensure that their atrocities terrorize others. Rejali himself cites the case of Abed Hamed Mowhoush, a captured Iraqi general who was beaten and placed in stress positions on display in front of the inmate population. Elsewhere he argues that "selective violence" has the effect of silencing dissent overall:

"Where violence is selective, people assume the right people are being targeted and this discourages anyone, enemy or not, from doing anything that might make them fall under suspicion. Death squads are chillingly effective even if they are not accurate."

But, of course, this general deterrence relies on the violence being broadly known. How do we understand such cases, absent the idea of public intimidation?

Rejali's commitment to the individuation of punishment is his inheritance from Foucault, who argued that the distinguishing characteristic of modern penal systems was their favoring of individual confinement to instill discipline and reform the inmate's

character, rather than using public demonstrations of physical violence to create a sort of awestruck respect for the might of the state.

The historical narrative of *Torture and Democracy* complicates Foucault's account considerably, since it highlights the persistence of corporal punishments in the contexts of military discipline, colonialism, and slavery and then carries them forward into modern police, prison, and military practices. Rejali, then, switches between the theory of individual intimidation and that of public terror without acknowledging the tension between the two, and without attempting to explain how one can translate into the other.

There is a real puzzle here, and it relates directly to Rejali's core thesis: How can the state both deny that it is using torture *and* use the threat of torture to terrorize the public (or, simultaneously— to present itself as a heroic protector)?

The answer, as I have said elsewhere, is that we do not have to *know* what happens to people in prison as long as we *suspect* enough to fear it. Privileged members of society may even draw comfort from such suspicions, especially if they never have to witness the violence or face the victims directly.

Torture exists in purported democracies as something of an open secret. We simultaneously know about torture and do not know about it. The state threatens it and denies it. We fear it, or relish it, and we pretend that it isn't happening. Sartre would call this "bad faith." Orwell called it "doublethink." Rejali prefers Bourdieu's term "*méconnaissance*"—"misrecognition."

> "Misrecognition ('*méconnaissance*') is the sociological process by which people habitually pass off one kind of situation as another. For life to go on, we proceed in this way. People misrecognize because they are invested in the particular way they think about themselves and others. Any other way of proceeding would be unthinkable or, at least, deeply disconcerting. . . . People partner in confirming each other's misrepresentation of the world, even if one person ends up somewhat worse off than before."

Rejali, of course, engages in his own misrecognition, accepting at face value the claim of some states—specifically Western imperial powers—to embody democracy, even as he accumulates evidence to the contrary.

How Monitoring Works, and Why It Fails

All states rule by force, and all states need legitimacy. Of course different types of states use force differently and establish and maintain their legitimacy in different ways. But the basic task of state-building is the challenge of legitimizing monopolistic violence.

States need coercion and public support; torture is seen as a good source of one, but it can undermine the other. Human rights monitoring works, when it does, by exploiting this contradiction and disrupting the illusion of state benevolence.

Organizations like Amnesty International and Human Rights Watch document government abuses, draw public attention to them, and work to make them undeniable. Such operations put the lie to the official rhetoric about human rights and freedom, they undercut the creditability of political leaders, and they call into question the state's claims of legitimacy. In short, they show how little the government can rely on the consent of the public, and how much it rules by force. Even totalitarian states see this as a problem. Monitoring can check abuses to the degree that it costs the government something that it needs, whether that be legitimacy, or allies, or funding, or public cooperation.

States that want to avail themselves of torture *and* maintain their claims to legitimacy will try to find ways to avoid the monitoring. The U.S., for example, is currently using several approaches—employing clean techniques like those Rejali describes; denying monitors access to inmates; hiding prisoners, sometimes in secret facilities; and outsourcing torture to other governments, local militias, or private mercenary firms. At the same time, the U.S. is perpetually trying to redefine torture, reinterpret its own laws, and rewrite the rules of war.

The main effect of monitoring, then, has been to push torture into invisibility, leading states to prefer "clean" methods over scarring methods, secret prisons over the public scaffold. Progress, in principle, has expanded norms of humane treatment and respect for rights, while in practice it has meant only less visible violence and more subtle cruelty. And even this meager sort of gain may prove to be temporary. Rejali writes:

"The question is whether a superpower can, by its own actions, undermine an international regime such as global human rights monitoring. . . . The answer is uncertain, but this study suggests that much depends on whether the state in question is a democracy or not. . . . Specific, credible information and appeals to rights can shake public confidence, influence policymakers, and raise questions about government policy and legitimacy. The United States can evade human rights auditing, even damage it considerably, but as long as it is a democracy, it is unlikely to be impervious to such pressures."

Perhaps this is meant to be reassuring. It reads to me more like an open question: To what degree is the United States a democracy, after all? The measure may be, in effect, whether or not it proves susceptible to this sort of pressure. The evidence, especially since 2001, is not encouraging.

What, then, should we do? On this always-crucial question, Rejali is oddly silent. The implicit answer would seem to be more and better monitoring, though he admits that "Stealth torture has disempowered ordinary observers, making monitoring a battle among experts"; and anyway, by his very thesis, the government will likely respond to improved monitoring by finding cleaner and sneakier modes of torture.

Rejali's answer, or non-answer, fits the overall pattern of his intellectual approach—specifically his focus on the technical at the expense of the political. For the successful abolition of torture will have less to do, surely, with advances in forensic medicine than with broad social changes—real shifts in political power, reduced stratification and greater equality, a move away from punitive conceptions of justice, and the dismantling of the institutions of violence.

In this sense, perhaps it *is* democracy that is at issue: The end of torture may well require the creation of real democracy.

Second Thoughts on Psychological Torture:
a review of *Torture and Democracy*, by Darius Rejali (Princeton University Press, 2007).

(*Make/Shift*, Spring/Summer 2009).

Torture doesn't have to leave scars. Governments are increasingly turning away from cuts and burns toward more discrete—but no less painful—practices like electroshock, forced standing, and partial drowning.

In *Torture and Democracy*, Darius Rejali carefully traces the development and transfer of "clean" (as opposed to "scarring") torture techniques during the past hundred-plus years. Covering nearly 600 pages of text, Rejali details the uses of the techniques mentioned above, as well as others like sleep deprivation, clean beating, exhaustion exercises, and narcosis.

But he ignores—even discounts—a whole range of psychological tortures, including the use of threats, prolonged isolation, and sexual humiliation. This approach doesn't just artificially truncate the category of "torture" but also obscures the gendered dynamics involved in its use.

A Narrow Definition

Rejali defines torture as "the systematic infliction of physical torment on detained individuals by state officials for police purposes, for confession, information, or intimidation."

There are several problems with this. First, Rejali tries to settle *as a matter of definition* empirical questions about who tortures and why. The result is a definition that excludes from the category of "torture" a great many things better off kept in: the use of cattle prods to control demonstrators; death squad atrocities; and practices that meet all the criteria, except that they are used for extortion, punishment, revenge, fun, or for racist or chauvinist reasons not endorsed by the law.

His tight definition does not fit his analysis of the spread of torture techniques. He suggests that torture is only a state activity, though he later describes the same techniques being used by the church, by slave-owners, and so on. He blocks consideration of the use of such techniques as punishment, though the history he outlines shows many of them *originated* as punishments for soldiers, sailors, and slaves.

And he just defines away the entire category of psychological torture. He writes:

"There are good reasons to keep the commonplace distinction between psychological fears and physical pain, not the least being that one would want to distinguish between torture and frivolous sentimental claims. If one does not distinguish between psychological fears of pain and pain itself, it is just as logical to argue that an uncomfortable thought counts as torture as it is to argue that sticking someone's head under water is simply playing on their psychological fears of death. And when torture becomes such a slippery word, analytic discussion becomes meaningless."

This argument is odd, when on the very next page, he says:

"modern torturers favor pains, physical or psychological, that intimidate the prisoner alone. At times, they reach farther than mere behavioral compliance, seeking to apply physical pain in order to touch the mind or warp a sense of self, and thereby shape the self-understanding of prisoners and dispose them to willing, compliant action."

If the point of torture is coercion or intimidation, by Rejali's analysis the mind of the victim is the real target and the body is merely the medium through which the state works. His "commonplace distinction" obscures this important fact, and misconstrues the ways torture is practiced. He seems to forget how many of the *physical* techniques he discusses work chiefly through fear, stress, and shame, rather than through the pain *per se*.

A 1963 CIA manual advises:

"The threat of coercion usually weakens or destroys resistance more effectively than coercion itself. . . . The threat to inflict pain, for example, can trigger fears more damaging than the immediate sensation of pain. . . . Sustained long enough, a strong fear of anything vague or unknown induces [psychological] regression, whereas materialization of the fear, the infliction of some form of punishment, is likely to come as a relief. The subject finds that he can hold out, and his resistance is strengthened."

By this account, it is the psychological pressure that does the work and physical pain is practically incidental—at best avoided, not from mercy, but to prolong the suffering.

Naturally, one must draw lines to conduct any sort of analysis. Not all suffering is torture, after all. But since Rejali spends several pages (especially 524-6) worrying over what torture does to the *perpetrators*, the psychological trauma of victims might merit at least as much concern.

Only Psychological?

Rejali admits that "Many a prisoner has been shattered by screams nearby, especially when they imagined they were hearing screams of loved ones," and he acknowledges that "all physical techniques of torture, clean or scarring, have psychological as well as physical effects." But he argues that

"clean techniques are not psychological techniques at all . . . [because] psychological techniques of coercion have for the most part only psychological effects."

Rejali doesn't just minimize the emotional suffering—that is, the "uncomfortable thought"—produced by prolonged isolation, mock execution, and rituals of humiliation. He also ignores the *physical* health effects of the psychological techniques. The scientific evidence suggests that, even by his narrow "physical torment" criterion, Rejali is wrong to omit consideration of many psychological tactics.

In their 2005 report, *Break Them Down*, Physicians for Human Rights documents both the persistent mental health effects and the long-term, painful, *physical* health consequences of psychological tortures. The report specifically addresses three types of torture that Rejali neglects—"Threats to Induce Fear of Death or Injury" (pages 54-5), "Sexual Humiliation" (55-9), and

"Solitary Confinement" (60-69). It notes the multiple symptoms experienced by torture victims:

"Some researchers . . . have argued for the creation of a specific 'torture syndrome,' distinguished by memory and concentration impairment, sleep disturbance and nightmares, susceptibility to emotional instability (emotional liability), anxiety, depression, and somatic complaints, including gastrointestinal, cardiopulmonary, and sympathetic distress.

Others have argued that torture survivors suffer from complex PTSD, or disorders of extreme stress, which are characterized by depression, impairment in mood regulation, sexual disturbances, amnesia, dissociative disorder, depersonalization, feelings of guilt and shame, self-accusation, self-mutilation, suicidality, excessive fantasies of revenge, disturbed perception of the perpetrator (idealization), social isolation, extreme mistrust, tendency for revictimization, hopelessness, despair, psychosomatic complaints, and conversion syndromes.

Survivors of torture often develop substance abuse problems as a means of suppressing traumatic memories and managing the anxiety that results from torture."

(Paragraph breaks added for clarity.) The paper also quotes the U.N. Special Rapporteur on torture:

"Almost invariably the effect of torture, by whatever means it may have been practiced, is physical and psychological. Even when the most brutal physical means are used, the long-term effects may be mainly psychological, even when the most refined psychological means are resorted to, there is nearly always the accompanying effect of severe physical pain."

Humiliation and Gender

These definitional issues are not mere intellectual quibbles or questions of rhetoric. They have genuine implications for how we understand—and how we respond to—torture. Misconceptions in this field threaten to have real political consequences.

It is striking, for example, that despite *Torture and Democracy's* extensive discussion of the Abu Ghraib scandal, it utterly neglects the aspect that was most discussed when the pictures first appeared—the systematic, stylized, sexual humiliation of the prisoners. Photographing men on leashes, or with women's underwear on their heads, or while they are forced to masturbate—these tactics, in Rejali's terms, would be merely psychological pressures and therefore not *really* torture. I'm sure Lynndie England would be relieved to hear it.

More troubling still, in the 551 pages of text, rape only receives the occasional passing mention (pages 78,148, and 486). Is this because Rejali considers rape (merely) psychologically painful, rather than physically painful? Or is it because it is not possible to track the techniques of sexual abuse in the same precise way as it is, say, partial drowning or electro-shock?

Either way—as a result of his narrow definition or his technique-focused methodology—Rejali obscures the gendered and gendering dynamics of an important and prominent torture method. And at the same time, he misses an opportunity to advance his own analysis.

He argues, in part, that clean techniques are useful because they allow a level of deniability—because the claims of the victims become unverifiable, because their accusations against the authorities devolve into contests of credibility, and because their friends and family are likely to question their virtue and challenge their failure to sufficiently resist.

Now, why does that dynamic sound so familiar?

Turning of the Imperialist Screw: Interview by Dave Mazza

(Portland Alliance, June 2006.)

Dave Mazza: In your first book, *Our Enemies in Blue: Police and Power in America*, you argue the importance of slavery to the development of our modern police institutions—that the police are very little about crime-solving and very much about social control. Did this nation's relationship with slavery play a similar role in the creation of places like Abu Ghraib?

Kristian Williams: There's some relevance, especially if you consider the historical connections between police and slavery and slavery and prisons in the U.S., and the evolution of the prison as a means of mass control, especially for the Black population. On the other hand, it's not simply reductive. The story isn't just "because we had slavery, we now have torture." Other factors are clearly important, especially U.S. imperialism.

Mazza: How does U.S. imperialism play a role?

Williams: The history of Guantánamo is pretty symbolic of this. It came under U.S. control in the Spanish-American War. The U.S. invaded Cuba. We then imposed a constitution on the island that put a lot of the country's resources under U.S. control. It guaranteed the right of U.S. intervention and turned over some strategic points for military bases—Guantánamo was one of those. Since that time it has been used—most recently and famously as an extralegal concentration camp for prisoners of war from Afghanistan and elsewhere.

Gitmo was chosen as the site for the prison on the theory that no law applies there. The Bush administration takes this line, anyway. But the base's lawless status actually dates from the Clinton administration, when it was used to detain Haitian refugees without considering their appeals for asylum.

Of course, the Supreme Court hasn't appreciated the Bush administration's legal arguments and U.N. has also launched an investigation into Gitmo. That sort of scrutiny internationally and in the U.S. is a main reason we took the further step of setting up secret prisons in Eastern Europe, Diego Garcia and elsewhere. But for that network, or Gitmo, to be there in the first place, there needed to be a background of the U.S. asserting control outside of its own territory and exempting itself from its own national laws. [. . .]

Mazza: You also raise the sexual nature of torture and its connection to sex and rape. Could you explain how those relationships work?

Williams: It's very complex, and I spend a whole chapter addressing this question. This got talked about quite a lot when the Abu Ghraib photos came out, but I realized in my research that it's common in these sort of abusive situations. Rape, sexual violence, and sexual humiliation just show up again and again—in Abu Ghraib, Guantánamo, and other military prisons, in domestic prisons, in the practices of our allies in the Middle East and in Latin America. It can't be a coincidence.

Part of the answer is technical. The torturer wants to hurt you as much as he can. The genitals are physically very sensitive, and sexuality is a sensitive area psychologically. So those become obvious targets. But on top of that, there's also the fact that in our society sex is all mixed up with ideas of violence and power. And sexual violence in particular is a major feature of the way that men dominate women. What I realized, writing the book, is that this actually says something fundamental about the way that power operates, and about how our society is organized.

In men's prisons, rape isn't just an expression of dominance, it's a way of organizing the inmate population, of stratifying it. Rape and sexual violence are used to create gender differences. And, upon reflection, it seems like that's just a replication of similar dynamics in the larger society. I find that very troubling.

Mazza: Work by Stanley Milgram and the Stanford Prison Experiment touch upon key issues in explaining why people permit torture to occur and even participate in it. Could you discuss that as well as talk about how we deal with those aspects of human nature?

Williams: Milgram's experiment was ingeniously simple. He asked volunteers to administer an electric shock to an innocent person. The "shock" was rigged to a buzzer and the "victim" was an actor, but the volunteers had no way to know that. The researchers expected that most people would refuse, and then they could examine the common traits of the people who participated—with the idea that this would lead them to understand the psychology of people who commit real-life atrocities. As it turned out, no one refused and a large portion continued with the experiment all the way to the maximum voltage. This was true even of volunteers who suffered guilt and anxiety, and vocally objected. What Milgram found was that among ordinary adult Americans the habit toward obedience was very much over-developed.

The Stanford experiment was less scientific. It may not be right to call it an experiment, in the usual sense; it's more like a well-documented anecdote. Psychologists at Stanford University set out to replicate prison conditions on the university's campus, and they did too good of a job. They randomly sorted a group of male students into prisoners and guards, and within hours the guards started mistreating the prisoners. After a few days things got so out of hand that the whole project had to be scrapped. It's interesting though—soldiers in the U.S. military have reported the same thing happening in their trainings to resist capture.

If we look at the two studies together—the Milgram study shows that normal people will do terrible things if ordered to do so by the authorities, and the Stanford study suggests that when given total control over others, ordinary people will indulge their most sadistic impulses. In real-world prisons, where both conditions are present to a greater or lesser degree, it's only too obvious what the results will be.

Mazza: You seem less optimistic at the close of this book. Can we get ourselves out of this fix and if so, how?

Williams: In *Our Enemies in Blue*, I really stressed what is possible. In *American Methods*, I focus more on what is necessary. In each book I was pressing against the usual boundaries of the debate.

Talking about the police, it's usual to assume that whatever their flaws, we have to have them. I argue otherwise, taking seriously the idea that we could eliminate this institution and find other, better, means of insuring public safety.

When talking about torture, human rights advocates tend to base their arguments on international law— really understating the kind of changes necessary to actually eliminate this set of practices. So in *American Methods* I argue that if we really want to end torture, and not just forbid it, we need to radically alter, or very likely, dismantle the institutions that employ it. That means getting serious about abolishing prisons and police, and ending our government's imperialist military and global economic policies. Furthermore, it means correcting the power imbalances that give these organizations and policies their shape— racism, capitalism, and the dominance of men over women.

Ultimately, if we really want to eliminate torture, we need to break up the existing concentrations of power and press all of society in the direction of greater equality.

Dave Mazza is a former editor of The Portland Alliance.

Caging Race & Gender: a review of *Are Prisons Obsolete?* by Angela Y. Davis (Seven Stories Press, 2003).

(*Against the Current*, January/February 2005.)

In her latest book, *Are Prisons Obsolete?*, Angela Davis lays out the facts about incarceration, citing the current numbers, outlining the history of the prison system, and identifying the race, class and gender dynamics underpinning the prison boom. She explains the economics of the punishment industry and deconstructs the ideology supporting it.

More importantly, she forces us to consider radical change, and clears the ground for an agenda based not on reforms of the current system, but on a vision of a society where no one is caged.

Race and gender are in the fore of the analysis, and Davis runs the argument in both directions. By describing prison as a site where these systems of inequality intersect, she casts light on the nature and function of the prison system; but by describing the prison in these terms she also shows us something about the society that relies so heavily on incarceration. The discussion is shifted away from questions about crime and punishment and toward concerns for social justice and human rights.

The racial aspects of the analysis will largely be familiar to anyone who has thought seriously about prisons before—the over-representation of people of color, the historical similarities between prison and plantation, and so on. But some startling insights appear in the chapter "How Gender Structures the Prison System."

Davis situates women's prisons on a continuum of other disciplining mechanisms, including mental institutions and domestic violence. Unfortunately, this analysis is largely asymmetrical: We see how gender norms inform the treatment of female prisoners and their experience of incarceration, but there is no account of the implications of gender for male prisoners, though Davis seems to promise one. ("The title of this chapter is not 'Women and the Prison System,' but rather 'How Gender Structures the Prison System'.") She shows us how gender-specific standards influence the women's prison system, but doesn't explain how similar standards influence men's prisons. The result is one-half of what could be a very illuminating comparison.

In terms of the history, Davis' Marxist tendencies lie close to the surface. It is the prison's relationship to capitalism that really drives the narrative. At every opportunity, the book highlights parallels between the prison's development and that of the capitalist economy.

Davis reminds us that *time* became the measure of punishment during the same period that it became the measure of labor. And the purpose of punishment was, theoretically, individual reform and discipline—a direct application of the Protestant ethic, well suited to the demands of an industrialized economy. She writes:

"If we combine [Protestant reformer John] Howard's emphasis on disciplined self-regulation with [utilitarian philosopher Jeremy] Bentham's ideas regarding the technology of internalization designed to make surveillance and discipline the purview of the individual prisoner, we can begin to see how such a conception of the prison had far-reaching implications. The conditions of possibility for this new form of punishment were strongly anchored in a historical era during which the working class needed to be constituted as an army of self-disciplined individuals capable of performing the requisite labor for a developing capitalist system."

Davis then brings the economic analysis up to date, explaining how profits are sucked out of the prison system, as private companies take over prison management, exploit prison labor, and sell their wares in prison markets:

"Thus, the prison industrial complex is much more than the sum of all the jails and prisons in this country. It is a set of symbiotic relationships among correctional communities, transnational corporations, media conglomerates, guards' unions, and legislative and court agendas."

The Life Cycle of Prisons

Broadly speaking, we could say Davis' book outlines the prison system's life cycle. It recounts the prison's birth during the early capitalist period, describes its growth into a mature prison industrial complex, and forecasts its death in the course of further social change.

Davis stresses the real possibility of change—she insists on it—and she urges the readers to work out for themselves what, precisely, a better world would look like: "The most difficult and urgent challenge today is that of creatively exploring new terrains of justice, where the prison no longer serves as our major anchor."

Rather than simply delineating alternatives to incarceration, she explains how to think creatively about such alternatives. This is by far the stronger approach, for it does not wrongly suggest easy solutions but instead pushes readers outside the accepted ideological framework and forces them to confront the real questions surrounding the demands of justice. In one way, the book itself is a liberating force, unlocking our critical thinking, our moral sense, and—perhaps most importantly—our imaginations.

Critical Resistance at 10: Addressing Abolition, Violence, Race, and Gender

(Against the Current, March/April 2009.)

On the weekend of September 26-28 [2008], 3,500 people gathered in Oakland, California to hasten the death of the prison system.

Marking the tenth anniversary of the prison-abolition group Critical Resistance, this conference, "CR-10," drew a diverse assemblage from around the country—diverse in terms of age, race, gender, sexuality, and political experience.

Activists, scholars, and former prisoners were all represented—three categories by no means mutually exclusive. Comprising three days of workshops, discussions, and films, the conference promised to assess the first ten years of the organization, evaluate present conditions, and consider future directions for the movement.

At present there are 2.3 million people in American prisons or jails. Whether measured in numerical terms or on a *per capita* basis, this is more than any other country. And it is seven times as many as in 1970.

Most of these prisoners are people of color: 40% are Black and 20% Hispanic. A Black man has a 32% chance of being incarcerated; an Hispanic man has a 17% chance; for a white man, the figure is 6%. This fact suggests one function of mass incarceration: the defense of white supremacy in the post-civil rights era.

As the prison system has expanded, as it has become increasingly integral to both our political and economic systems, as it has developed into what CR calls "the Prison-Industrial Complex"—the idea of abolition has become simultaneously more remote and more important.

In 1998, Critical Resistance became a national organization almost by accident. As one of the founders, Ruthie Gilmore, explained it to me, CR started as a loose coalition of people who were already fighting the prison system; they decided to host a conference called "Critical Resistance," and ended up forming the organization that inherited that name.

Since then CR has grown to an organization with hundreds of members and branches in nine cities. CR has shifted the discussion among activists, establishing abolition as a legitimate point on the political continuum. It also challenges us to find other solutions to crime.

These two contributions became the largest preoccupations of the CR-10 conference, from what I saw: uncertainty about the relationship between prison reform and prison abolition, and the search for alternatives to incarceration.

Tony Platt, a criminologist and one of the organizers of the 1972 "Tear Down the Walls" conference, remembers:

"The prison movement of the early seventies paid almost no attention to crime. Crime was romanticized as a sort of pre-political form of rebellion. . . . The issue of violence within communities was not given a priority."

This naiveté cost the movement dearly, allowing the right wing to monopolize the issue of crime, leveraging it for political support and using it to reframe issues of poverty and race.

Tensions With Feminism

Worse still, in the '70s, at exactly the time when feminists were pressing the authorities to take violence against women seriously, the anti-prison movement largely ignored the experience of survivors of crime.

Tensions between the anti-racist and feminist strands of the left were exacerbated, and feminist strategy increasingly came to rely on state intervention. Platt credits the 2001 "Critical Resistance/Incite Statement on Gender Violence and the Prison Industrial Complex" for trying to re-align the two tendencies.

That statement, jointly released by the two organizations, begins:

"We call on social justice movements to develop strategies and analysis that address both state and interpersonal violence, particularly violence against women. . . . It is critical that we develop responses to gender violence that do not depend on a sexist, racist, classist, and homophobic criminal justice system. It is also important that we develop strategies that challenge the criminal justice system and that also provide safety for survivors of sexual and domestic violence."

The statement goes on to enumerate the many ways both the anti-prison movement and the mainline feminist movement have—largely because of the fissure between them—marginalized women of color.

On the one hand, "the mainstream anti-violence movement has increasingly relied on the criminal justice system" without fully considering the impact of increased policing and incarceration on communities of color.

On the other hand,

"because . . . [prison abolitionists] have not always centered gender and sexuality in their analysis or organizing, we have not always responded adequately to the needs of survivors of domestic and sexual violence."

Women of color inhabit an intersection between racism and sexism, so analyses that only focus on one type of oppression tend to leave them out.

Feminists cannot afford to forget about racism, and they cannot rely on racist institutions. They need to consider the way the state reproduces inequality and examine the real effects of a state-centered strategy. At the same time, prison abolitionists cannot be sanguine about crime, or ignore its victims; they must find alternate solutions to violence and help ensure community safety.

By pushing for dialogue, the CR/Incite statement greatly benefited both of the movements it addressed, making clear the absolute need for an analysis that takes account of race *and* gender. Such an analysis needs to address both interpersonal and state violence. The statement, while rightly critical of the two movements, actually provided a basis for unity: It demonstrated that the feminist anti-violence movement and the anti-prison movement share a common task.

Indeed it seems that the anti-prison movement has taken the challenge seriously. Of the 167 workshops listed in the CR-10 program, 13 dealt in a direct way with finding alternatives to incarceration and other state violence. These included: an Incite workshop specifically for people of color on "Community-Based Responses to Violence;" a presentation by the Audre Lorde Project on their efforts to use "community accountability strategies" to address both hate crimes and police brutality; a roundtable discussion on existing alternatives in place in California; a presentation by Creative Interventions on "Community Accountability Strategies for Intimate Violence;" and a workshop by Generation Five on responses to child sexual abuse. Of course, the question of alternatives also arose in workshops not specifically focused on the issue.

Facing Hard Questions

Yet while talk about long-term strategies and the need to develop alternatives was spotlighted, consideration of immediate reforms has been sidelined. This ambivalence is similarly reflective of lessons drawn from past mistakes. After all, the modern penitentiary was itself started by reformers—promoted as a humane alternative to corporal punishment.

More recently, the drive to eliminate indeterminate sentencing began as a reform effort and produced the policy disaster of mandatory minimums. Naneen Karraker, one of the organizers of the 1998 Critical Resistance conference, looks back on that effort with regret: "In retrospect, [it was] a very bad decision, because rather than having fewer people in prison for a shorter time, the legislators made it so that there were more for a longer time."

There is always the danger that reforms will extend the life of the institution, add to its legitimacy, or even increase its power. How do you balance that against the chance to alleviate some portion of the real suffering experienced by people who are in prison now?

One workshop was provocatively titled, "Are the fight for reform and the fight for abolition mutually exclusive?" During the session, a young Black woman working for reforms said, "I'm looking for real-world advice, not just CR-10 conference advice, on how we accomplish the just, not just the possible."

There are hard questions, questions that cannot be neatly put aside with platitudes or abstractions. At the opening plenary, Andrea Smith of Incite advocated "revolution by trial and error," explaining "If we really knew how to end oppression we would have done it by now."

Angela Davis called for both hope and urgency. She argued that, despite the increasing numbers of prisoners,

"we've moved further toward the goal of prison abolition. . . . We have come a long way in the last ten years. But we are not yet there. And so impatience is important. *Impatience.*"

She concluded:

"Abolition is not a never-to-be-realized utopian dream of the future. Abolition is our collective practice. So we say, Abolition Now, Abolition Now, *Abolition Now!*"

Part Five:
Conclusions and Synopses

What Anarchism Contributes To Our Understanding of Torture:

Comments delivered at the Anarchist Book Fair, San Francisco; March 23, 2008

(Social Anarchism, 2008-2009.)

As I was preparing this talk, it occurred to me that I don't think I used the word "anarchism" anywhere in the two hundred-plus pages of American Methods. That's somewhat ironic, since I consider the analysis of the book to be anarchistic from top to bottom. So I'm going to speak for a few minutes about what anarchism contributes to our understanding of torture.

It will help if we consider the standard analyses of torture. The crudest of these focus on individual personalities, whether it's the perverse soap opera of Lynndie England's love affair with Charles Graner, or Donald Rumsfeld's squabbles with his own generals, or George W. Bush's rather tenuous relationship with reality. At the next level of analysis, we get discussions of particular instruments, like tasers, or techniques, like water-boarding. After that, we see discussion of more institutional aspects, such as policies or training. And at the most abstract, there is the tension between executive power and the rule of law.

Now all of that's worth looking at, and some remarkable work has been

done on those questions. But what's missing, from all these discussions, is the role of the state as such.

That's rather surprising, and it shouldn't just surprise anarchists. The Absolutist philosopher Thomas Hobbes would have likely been surprised at the limited attention the state receives, since he saw force as the defining characteristic of the state and the law merely as the codification of the sovereign's will. Even by Max Weber's definition—the basic definition accepted by most social scientists—states monopolize force. One would think, then, that state power is precisely the issue.

So, why is the state missing?

There are two main reasons. The first is the broad acceptance of liberal assumptions about government, namely that it is inevitable, permanent, and legitimate. The state is taken for granted to the point of being forgotten. It is assumed, and thereby obscured. It's everywhere, and therefore gets overlooked.

The second reason concerns our historical amnesia and our post-9/11 tunnel vision. We've forgotten the history of torture before September 11, 2001. Because we're encouraged to think of torture as special to our circumstances—especially the War on Terror—it becomes hard to recognize the continuities in its use, both from earlier periods of time, and as these continuities exist between the use of torture abroad and the practices of police and prisons domestically. As a result, we misunderstand the role of the institutions involved—prisons, police, the military.

There are real consequences to these sorts of mistakes. Because torture is largely viewed as a unique feature of the Bush administration, or of the War on Terror, the proposed solutions tend to involve either a change of leadership or a return to the rule of law. The Democrats, of course, emphasize leadership. Human rights organizations and lawyers focus on the rule of law. But the truth is that neither is likely to be enough.

Anarchism understands that torture is not simply a matter of bad people doing bad things. It's a function of power and the institutions that wield it—especially the state. Because anarchism puts the focus back on the state, it can account for the historical continuity of torture practices, and for the similarity of abuses domestically and abroad.

So while liberals and genuine conservatives are surprised and appalled by the lawlessness of Guantánamo, anarchists see it as exemplifying state power. It's exactly the sort of thing that we would expect. Hence we won't look for salvation from the Democrats, or the courts, or the U.N. To stop torture we have to break down the institutions responsible for it. We have to do away with the police, the prisons, the military, the spy agencies—the whole coercive apparatus of government.

By putting the focus back on the state, anarchism makes torture explicable, and offers a genuine path toward its elimination rather that wishful thinking about human rights and empty promises concerning the rule of law. It also understands the necessity of struggle. Because it is the nature of power to expand, we can never settle for a barely-tolerable *status quo*. The choice is not between a better future, or more of the same. Without resistance, things inevitably get worse.

Five Theses on Violence

(The Body as a Site of Discrimination: Exploring and Resisting Body-Based Oppressions, April 17, 2009.)

I begin by offering five related propositions:

1) If inequality relies on violence, then the body is necessarily a site of discrimination.

2) If the body is a site of discrimination, then it is also a (potential) site of resistance, of struggle.

3) If the body is a site of struggle, then it is not only the bodies of the victims, but the bodies of the perpetrators, that are at issue.

4) The state, by claiming a monopoly on the legitimacy of violence, in effect declares certain bodies to be legitimate instruments of violence, and certain bodies to be legitimate targets.

5) If we look at the bodies that suffer sanctioned violence, we can gain important information about the organization of social inequality.

I believe that these are relatively modest claims, and each, I think, can stand on its own. But I offer them here, together, in the form of an argument because I want to articulate the connections between them. I want to make the underlying logic stand out.

The first statement begins with a supposition that inequality relies on violence—at least sometimes. I should specify here that by "violence" I do not mean anything vague or abstract, like "emotional violence" or "economic violence." I mean physical force used against beings capable of experiencing injury and pain—in short: hitting, kicking, stabbing, burning, shooting, and the like. Historically, this type of behavior has been one of the ways people with power respond to demands for increased equality, so I do not expect this supposition to prove very controversial.

Since by "violence" we mean *physical* violence (and, in particular, physical violence against sentient beings, and not mere things), the second clause clearly follows from its antecedent. Violence, in the relevant sense, is necessarily applied to the body; if it is done in the defense, or for the furtherance, of inequality, then the site of the violence is *ipso facto* a site of discrimination.

This conclusion becomes the premise of the second thesis, from which it is suggested that the body is also a potential locale for resistance. Sometimes people deliberately *expose* their bodies to violence as a challenge to inequality: civil rights demonstrators facing firehoses and police dogs in Birmingham, Republican prisoners on hunger strike in Northern Ireland, slaves engaging in self-mutilation and suicide. Other times, they *remove* their bodies from the violence: this is the strategy of refugees, fugitives, runaways, and deserters. And sometimes people *fight back*—fight, not in the metaphorical or political sense, but literally, responding to violence with violence.

It is with violent resistance that another set of bodies suddenly comes into focus—the bodies of the perpetrators. The third thesis reminds us that violence is not only an instrument of inequality and discrimination; it can also be a means of resisting them. And likewise, violence is not simply something that *happens* to the bodies of its victims; it is also something that other people *do* using their own bodies. It will be noted that the perpetrator/victim distinction is too simple, because the same bodies that inflict violence can also be made to suffer it.

The fourth thesis offers an elaboration of the third, building from Weber's famous definition of the state as a set of institutions that claim a monopoly on legitimate violence within a given territory. *Legitimacy*, of course, presumes a kind of discrimination —between authorized and unauthorized *uses* of violence, but also between those *bodies* the state authorizes to do violence and those it does not, and between those bodies against whom the state authorizes

violence as opposed to those it protects. Discriminations, we should remember, are not strictly dichotomies; they exist as matters of degree, are often relative, and may shift with context or circumstance.

The fifth, and final, statement presents an empirical question—*What sorts of bodies suffer authorized violence?*— and articulates its relevance to the broader understanding of social stratification. The bodies that experience "legitimate" (especially state) violence are themselves a type of evidence concerning the nature of inequality in a given society.

In our society, in the United States at the beginning of the twenty-first century, some of this evidence is readily available: In the country as a whole, 1,057 people were executed during the period 1977-2006. Of these poisoned, electrocuted, or suffocated bodies, 33% were Black—a strikingly disproportionate number, given that only 11.1% (in 1970) to 12.3% (in 2000) of the total population was Black. The numbers representing more routine violence are harder to come by, but the Bureau of Justice Statistics does offer this:

"Blacks (4.4%) and Hispanics (2.3%) were more likely than whites (1.2%) to experience the use of force during contact with police in 2005. Blacks accounted for 1 out of 10 contacts with police, but 1 out of 4 contacts where force was used."

The state is, in many respects, an easy target. But if one wants to understand inequality in society at large, one must also investigate our other institutions, especially those where violence is, if not precisely authorized, then at least tolerated, condoned, or ignored by the relevant authorities. What sorts of bodies are hurt in the nation's schools? in its mental hospitals and drug treatment centers? in nursing homes? in the churches? in the family? What sorts of inequalities do these injuries reveal?

Talking about *bodies* is useful because it helps to remind us that politics is not only about abstract principles and broad social forces. It is also personal, and physical. But there is a danger in this rhetoric, as well. It has become faddish, of late, to write about "bodies" in ways that sometimes obscure the fact that we are really talking about *people*. A person is more than her body. A person is also her emotions, her beliefs, her memories, her imagination, her capacities, and her range of activity. Treating a person as a body often involves some degree of violence. Reducing a person to a body always does.

My argument began with a hypothetical: "*If inequality relies on violence . . .*" I believe that it does—at least some inequality, at least some of the time. But inequality does not *only* rely on violence, it is not only exercised through violence, and it is not only visible in violence. We would do well to consider what else it relies on, and how else it can be resisted.

Power does not only operate on our bodies, and the use it makes of our bodies is—even in extreme cases, such as torture—often but a means for imposing on our interior worlds. For power seeks to shape, mobilize, and exploit, not just our bodies, but our desires, fears, insecurities, loyalties, values, creativity—our whole selves. These elements—which characterize both our individuality and our shared humanity—may also be seen as sites of struggle, and may provide a basis for resistance.

About the Author

Kristian Williams is the author of *American Methods: Torture and the Logic of Domination* and *Our Enemies in Blue: Police and Power in America* (both from South End Press), as well as another short collection, *Confrontations: Selected Journalism* (Tarantula, 2007).

Kristian lives in Portland, Oregon, and is a member of Rose City Copwatch.

BE OUR "BEST FRIEND FOREVER"

Do you love what Microcosm publishes?
Do you want us to publish more great stuff?
Would you like to receive each new title as
it's published?

If you answer "*yes!*" then you should subscribe
to our BFF program. BFF subscribers help
pay for printing new books, zines, and more.
They also ensure that we can continue to
print great material each month! Every time
we publish something new we'll send it to
your door!

Subscriptions are based on a sliding scale
of $10-30 per month. Please give what you
can afford so that we can be sure to send
out more stuff each month. Include your
t-shirt size and month/date of birthday for
a possible surprise!

microcosmpublishing.com/bff

Minimum subscription period is 6 months. Subscription begins the month after
it is purchased. To receive more than 6 months, add multiple orders to your
quantity.

Microcosm Publishing
636 SE 11th Ave. Portland, OR 97214
www.microcosmpublishing.com